COACH YOURSELF BETTER, FAST

HOW TO GET TO KNOW YOUR CUSTOMER

Based on *Do Penguins Eat Peaches?* by Katie Tucker

First published in Great Britain by Practical Inspiration Publishing, 2025

© Katie Tucker and Practical Inspiration Publishing, 2025

The moral rights of the author have been asserted.

ISBN 978-1-78860-756-8 (paperback)
      978-1-78860-757-5 (epub)
      978-1-78860-758-2 (Kindle)

All rights reserved. This book, or any portion thereof, may not be reproduced without the express written permission of the publisher.

Every effort has been made to trace copyright holders and to obtain their permission for the use of copyright material. The publisher apologizes for any errors or omissions and would be grateful if notified of any corrections that should be incorporated in future reprints or editions of this book.

EU GPSR representative: LOGOS EUROPE, 9 rue Nicolas Poussin, LA ROCHELLE 17000, France Contact@logoseurope.eu

Want to bulk-buy copies of this book for your team and colleagues? We can customize the content and co-brand *How to Get to Know Your Customer* to suit your business's needs.

Please email info@practicalinspiration.com for more details.

Contents

Series introduction iv
Introduction 1
Day 1: Kill your assumptions 5
Day 2: Get curious 13
Day 3: Find your customers 20
Day 4: Understand your customers 25
Day 5: Ask your customers 34
Day 6: Make it make sense 46
Day 7: Become a digital spy 54
Day 8: Stop sending shitty surveys 64
Day 9: Test your ideas 75
Day 10: Turn insights into action 84
Conclusion 90
Endnotes 92

Series introduction

Welcome to *6-Minute Smarts*!

This is a series of very short books with one simple purpose: to introduce you to ideas that can make life and work better, and to give you time and space to think about how those ideas might apply to your life and work.

Each book introduces you to ten powerful ideas, but ideas on their own are useless – that's why each idea is followed by self-coaching questions to help you work out the 'so what?' for you in just six minutes of exploratory writing. What's exploratory writing? It's the kind of writing you do just for yourself, fast and free, without worrying what anyone else thinks. It's not just about getting ideas out of your head and onto paper where you can see them, it's about finding new connections and insights as you write. This is where the magic happens.

Find out more...

Introduction

How well do you know your customers? How often are you conducting market research with them? You're probably doing a yearly survey. Asking for feedback and reviews. Using social media to poll your followers. Checking usage data on your digital channels perhaps. You might be building customer knowledge organically as you go along. Maybe you're doing even more than this.

But are you asking your customers the right questions – questions that will help you make better decisions, create better content (we're all content creators these days) and build better products and services? Are you leveraging the latest technological advances to eavesdrop on public conversations? Are you taking advantage of all the free research available online? Probably not. Perhaps you don't know how and where to start.

How to Get to Know Your Customer

From my experience working with smaller businesses, I believe your relationship to market research is likely to fall into one of these three categories:

- You're doing it intuitively, in everything but name (you're probably a naturally good listener and an empath). Brilliant, but difficult to replicate and scale. Read on: the steps in this book will help you carve out a repeatable process from your natural qualities.
- You're doing some, but not really getting anything useful and struggling to see the value. This book will help you with the tools and skills to ensure you're getting valuable insights.
- You're not doing it at all. For you, the steps in this book will change everything.

Make small your superpower

Being a large business sure has its benefits: more people to do the work, more expertise and more money to spend. But remember: small can be incredibly powerful too when it comes to understanding customers. Small means you're closer to the people you serve. Small means faster decision-making. The Covid-19 pandemic highlighted the kindness and nimbleness of small businesses, which were quicker and more considerate to react to changing customer needs.

On the opposite end of the spectrum, big businesses are under scrutiny for all the wrong reasons. Tax avoidance. Unfair workplace practices. Greedy shareholders. Greenwashing. Data abuse. They're as popular as a wet summer weekend. Your business isn't like that. It's time to use small to your advantage.

Why market research matters

Market research has a serious image problem. Boring. Time-consuming. Dated. Colette Doyle, acting editor at the MRS (Market Research Society) quarterly magazine, *Impact*, hit the nail on the head in an editorial when she wrote: 'Whenever the term pops up... people... tend to picture a grizzled, white-haired gentleman with horn-rimmed glasses, brandishing a clipboard.'[1] But don't be fooled. Bigger brands are ALL over it. From leading supermarket chains to the ever-imposing tech giants, they're systematically and forensically trying to figure out every move with fancy teams and even fancier tools. And it's easy to see why. Every dollar invested in understanding customers brings a whopping $100 in return.[2]

How to Get to Know Your Customer

Bigger companies may be calling it something different. Something with a little more street cred. Customer insight. Customer discovery. Audience analysis. Customer research. User research (UX). Design research. Service design. Customer experience (CX). This book won't be splitting semantic hairs. The fact is understanding customers is an integral part of how successful businesses operate.

Businesses like yours need to do more. Can do more. Just enough more. So that you too can make smarter decisions, build more robust offerings, stay competitive and reduce the guessing. In just a few six-minute sessions, this book will teach you how.

You're ready to start. Over ten chapters (ten days, if you fancy treating this as a mini-course), you're going to discover ten key principles that will enable you to take a step back and notice what really matters in business: customers. This book will give you a chance to question what you believe to be true. You'll finish the book more curious and ready to build new habits that will help your customers and your business.

Let's go!

Day 1
Kill your assumptions

Let's get one thing straight. You may well have started your business to scratch your own itch. Maybe you launched a vegan cheese because you couldn't find one that didn't taste like soft plastic. Or you opened a high-end thrift store, tired of shrunken Primark T-shirts being sold for a fiver. Or you launched a coaching business following a transformational coaching experience of your own. This does not make you a know-it-all when it comes to your customers. Scratching your own itch can do loads of other useful things, like make it easy to connect with your first customers and help build some decent assumptions about what they could want. But don't mistake that for *actually* knowing what your customers want.

How to Get to Know Your Customer

The biggest mistake I see business owners make is thinking: 'I know my customer – they're just like me.' Until they're not. And it all ends in tears. The moment you step into entrepreneurship, your perception of what your customers want inevitably shifts, however much you had in common with them in the early days. You are just too invested in the outcome. And you can't use friends and family as a proxy for your customers. They may have been some of your first customers, but don't kid yourself – they were just being nice.

Your customers are real people. They're out there in the real world, living their messy, imperfect lives. If you want people to buy your stuff, you need to find them and talk to them so you can understand them better. As American entrepreneurs Steve Blank and Bob Dorf most famously wrote (repeatedly!) in *The Startup Owner's Manual*: 'You need to get out of the building.'[3] The rallying cry for businesses to go talk to customers is a simple, yet powerful, reminder of what truly matters. 'Facts only exist outside the building, where customers live', they say.[4]

Talking to real people is the most effective and powerful way to understand the people you serve. To understand the context in which they need and use your stuff. Is it uncomfortable? Sometimes. Can you get used to it? Absolutely. Can I teach you how? Hell, yes – just read on.

Assumptions kill dreams

If we're not getting out of the building (or our home office) to find customers to talk to, then how are we making our business decisions? We make assumptions. But in business, when we assume, we take a risk, a punt on something that may not be true.

An assumption is 'a belief or feeling that something is true or that something will happen, although there is no proof'.[5] Read those last two words out loud. *No proof*. Don't get me wrong, assumptions in business *can* be useful. They have foundations. They're built on our perception of reality as *we* see it and on how *we* experience the world. They are a great starting point and can evolve into hypotheses to be proved or disproved. But they need to be checked. Especially the BIG assumptions. The ones that carry the most risk in terms of time, money and precious energy.

Why are assumptions so appealing? Well, as humans, we can't sense-check everything. Our brains would implode. We assume the sun will rise tomorrow. That our car will start. That the plane we are about to take will land safely. That the world won't end next Sunday. Our brain is wired to look for shortcuts.

Managing assumptions is also a way of managing risks. The risk of the sun not rising is tiny, so we don't worry about it. The risk of the car not starting is low, so we don't check it over. The risk of being in a plane crash is small, so we take that plane. The risk of the world ending on Sunday is infinitesimal, so we don't even give it a second thought. What we are doing is assessing the risk of being wrong. If it's small enough, we don't bother checking. Seriously, a smart way to live.

In business, though, things aren't as simple. We glorify risk-takers and idolize rock star entrepreneurs. *Just Do It* has become our modern slogan. But let's not confuse being comfortable taking risks with letting assumptions alone guide our every business decision. Business is not a zero-risk game, and however much research you do, you can't eliminate all risks. But the successful businesses and entrepreneurs pick out their riskiest assumptions and check them. We are just rarely shown that side of the story.

Even the big guns sometimes get it wrong and launch things nobody wants (Google glasses, anyone?). But bigger companies can financially cushion their flops. As a small business owner,

Kill your assumptions

you have more to lose if you head too far down the wrong path.

So if assumptions are dangerous, what do we do to protect our businesses? Well, we check. We find out. We test. We discover and we question. Not just the once but as we go along, because things change. Customers are people and people change. Trends come and go, and global pandemics damage foundations we thought were unbreakable in our modern societies. Customers are a moving target, so we can't be complacent. We need to pay attention. Successful brands do just that. They evolve, innovate and move with the times. They use customer research as a tool to understand their audience and make changes when necessary.

And, from today, that's what you're going to do too.

So what? Over to you...

1. Think about a time when you made an incorrect assumption about your customer. What led you to believe it?

Kill your assumptions

2. Are you relying on friends, family or personal biases to define your customer? Why might that be dangerous?

3. Brain-dump all the assumptions you hold about your target customers, then go through the list and identify the ones that need checking.

Day 2
Get curious

Being an explorer in business means approaching things with a beginner's mind. It's that feeling you get when you step off a plane in a brand-new city, when you try a hobby for the very first time or when you find yourself in a room full of strangers. Approach customer understanding in the same way: with curiosity, empathy and a healthy dose of courage. You might not consider these qualities as tools in the traditional sense, but redefining them as such helps you apply them in business more efficiently. Curiosity, allied with courage, helps us move out of the nebulous realm of emotional to the realm of practicality.

Curiosity

When do we stop asking questions? Anyone who has been around a bunch of five-year-olds knows they ask a *lot* of questions. Research shows that small kids ask around 107 questions per hour.[6] As we grow up, this extraordinary number dwindles. Older children already ask fewer questions than their younger peers, and by the time we reach adulthood, our curiosity falls off a cliff. At its core, curiosity is asking questions, and asking questions is learning. As kids, we learn about the world around us by asking. Every answer we get shrinks our knowledge gap, so by the time we reach adulthood, we know enough to navigate the world and we stop asking (as many) questions.

Curiosity and market research go hand in hand. American author and anthropologist Zora Neale Hurston describes research as 'formalized curiosity. Poking and prying with purpose.'[7] Running a business is inviting your inner five-year-old back to stay. We're born curious and it's how we learn. We *can* be curious again. Diana Kander is a *New York Times* bestselling author, keynote speaker and curiosity expert. 'When it comes to understanding customers, curiosity is simply the gap between what you know and what you don't know,' she told me. Sounds obvious when

Get curious

you think about it, but the truth is very few of us wallow long enough in that space.

If I put you on the spot, you might not be able to articulate off the cuff your gaps in customer knowledge. But I guarantee questions naturally pop into your head on a regular basis (that's curiosity right there!). Why aren't my customers buying this? What format do my customers prefer when it comes to courses? Will customers still buy if I put my postage prices up? What do my customers find most useful?

Curiosity comes naturally to some of us. However, not every upbringing or work culture creates safe spaces for curiosity. Curiosity is the explorer's prize tool. Identifying knowledge gaps and asking questions to fill them is how we'll learn about customers. Practise curiosity at home and out in the wild. Make time for it. It will trickle back into your business behaviours soon enough. As an adult, being curious is a choice. Make it.

Courage

Along with curiosity, courage is an essential part of your business exploration toolkit. Courage is often elevated to superhuman feats and exceptional actions. The courage we need in business is quieter, out of the spotlight, but equally powerful. In a knowledge-is-power culture, it takes courage to admit we don't have all the answers. It takes courage to put our ideas out into the world with no guarantee of what we'll get back. When done right, market research is exposing. We test assumptions that we hold tight. We share our ideas with real people, and we get feedback we might not want to hear. Market research is a vulnerable sport. You might not feel very brave right now, but courage in business, like curiosity, is something you can practise.

We can't be curious and brave all the time. But we can aspire to use these tools more of the time, especially when it comes to customers. We'll all have different definitions of what that looks like depending on our starting point. For some, brave might be reaching out to a friendly customer for the first time to ask for 30 minutes of their time; for others, it will mean pitching for investment after a successful product launch. Find your flavour of brave and run with it.

So what? Over to you…

1. Every time a question arises this week, store it in your Question Bank. This is your starting point for taking curious action.

2. Become a professional people watcher. Go where your customers are, and jot down everything you notice. Are they rushing/alone/distracted/struggling/comparing prices online?

Get curious

3. What's one brave action you could take to get closer to your customers this week?

Day 3
Find your customers

To truly know our customer, we need to speak to real people – what Steve Blank refers to as 'getting out of the building'.[8] But now you're probably asking: where do I find these mythical people to speak to? Valid question. One I get asked *all* the time. I usually respond with another question: How many people do you know?

Me? A musician. A DJ. An actor. A broadsheet journalist. A GP. A semi-pro goalkeeper. A headteacher. A nurse. A dog trainer. A kidney surgeon. A TV presenter. A supermarket checkout agent. A cleaner. A social worker. A Spanish diplomat (who narrowly escaped Ukraine). A university lecturer. A campaigner. A falafel maker in my local mall. A CEO. An award-winning broadcaster. A French dog groomer. A village

Find your customers

mayor. A nursery worker. A job seeker. A tax avoider. An influencer with 200k+ followers. At a push... Bryan Ferry (story on request).

I could go on. My point? The average human knows 600 people. We are only ever six introductions away from someone else on this planet.⁹ Fact. Now we could debate the definition of 'know', but I bet you have people to speak to. You might just need a little help. Here are a few sources for customers (or target customers) to speak to:

1. Your current customers
2. Your lapsed customers
3. Your mailing list
4. Social media
5. Alumni (school, college, university, previous places of work, etc.)
6. Personal network (think: dog walker, school gate parents, Saturday football club, etc.)
7. Friends of friends

And, finally, close friends and family. Seriously, don't go there. Often, they will only tell you what you want to hear. They mean well so indulge them lightly (it's nice for them to feel involved, especially if they're forking out any cash to support you), but don't take their word as gospel. Keep them for support. A safe place to vent. But don't base your business strategy on what they think.

So please don't tell me you don't have anyone to reach out to.

 So what? Over to you...

1. Map your network. Mind-map all the networks/groups you're connected to, professionally and personally.

Find your customers

2. Who's in that network? Take six minutes to write down every name that comes to mind.

3. Pick five promising names that you will reach out to – and now read Day 4!

Day 4
Understand your customers

So now that you have a list of people to speak to, you might think you just need to go ahead and ask them for a call, right? Wrong. Well, partially. We'll cover that in Day 5, but for now let's take a small step back. Before we fix a meeting, we need to understand our customers' motivations so that we can ask them the right questions. Things can go wrong quite quickly when you don't cover this important step, as we're about to find out...

In the late 1990s, McDonald's got it wrong. Big time! The fast-food giant wanted to boost milkshake sales. It profiled and surveyed its milkshake punters. 'More flavours?' it asked. 'Why not!' the customers said. McDonald's introduced more flavours but sales flatlined.

How to Get to Know Your Customer

So, they called in the late Harvard professor, Clayton Christensen. His team spent two days watching and talking (think asking questions) to McDonald's shake shoppers. His findings? Customers bought milkshakes to do very specific *jobs*: offset a boring drive to work; keep their mouths and (one) hand busy; and keep their bellies full for longer.

Armed with this new insight, McDonald's made some changes. It introduced thicker milkshakes (these took longer to drink, and customers stayed full for longer) and a faster and more convenient checkout process (which suited busy commuters trying to get to work on time). Shake sales increased sevenfold.

Christensen used something called the JTBD (Jobs To Be Done) framework to understand what McDonald's customers were *hiring* the milkshake for. He asked the right questions and got insight that boosted the fast-food giant's bottom line.

So, what exactly is JTBD and how can you apply it to your business? JTBD is a lens through which we understand people. Over the years, it has revolutionized the way many successful businesses go about understanding their customers, but it rarely finds its way to smaller businesses. The BIG idea is that customers go about their days getting (or trying to get) stuff done. In their work and in their life. We

Understand your customers

call the stuff they're trying to get done *jobs*. A job can be deciding what shampoo to use, which car to buy or what to do with your kids on a wet weekend. A job can be to relax, fix the toilet seat, level up in French, find healthy food options on the go, make a boring commute more enjoyable or sort out your relationship. The American business strategist Anthony Ulwick is credited with first shaping the concept back in the 1990s. He has written (and still does write) extensively on the topic. However, more recently, JTBD is associated with the works and teachings (and milkshake musings) of Clayton Christensen.

This approach is ground-breaking because it reframes our products and services as things customers hire (think buy and use) to get *jobs* done. Once we figure out what jobs they're trying to get done by hiring a product or service (maybe ours, maybe someone else's), we can work out how to help them get that job done better, faster and more rewardingly. This isn't some business theory only relevant to the tech world or B2B (business-to-business) – this idea works for selling candles, watches, courses, cars and even toilet roll.

JTBD changes the way businesses ask questions from 'What do you want?' to 'What are you trying to get done?' Ultimately, jobs tend to last, while products don't. And over time, one job (listening to music, for example) will be satisfied via a myriad of solutions and products (gramophone, cassette player, turntable, CD, smart phones, Alexa...). Jobs theory allows you to innovate on the how without being tied to one single solution.

JTBD also helps us view our products and services beyond their functional use and encourages us to think about the other stuff that goes on (social and emotional factors) when making a purchase decision. Finally, JTBD shakes up how we view our competitors.

Beyond the functional

One of the most useful aspects of the JTBD theory is how it helps businesses embrace the social and emotional aspects of what drives consumer behaviour. This is important these days, as there are hundreds if not thousands of businesses offering essentially the same product. If everyone was choosing products based on their functional uses, there wouldn't be any need for so much choice. However, customers are humans, so emotions are always involved.

JTBD puts *jobs* into three main categories: functional jobs, emotional jobs and social jobs.

Understand your customers

Functional jobs are the easiest to grasp and the category we feel most comfortable exploring as small businesses (e.g. I buy a car to get from A to B). *Social* is all about how things make your customer look (in society) as a result of choosing a certain product to get a *job* done (e.g. I buy a Tesla for social kudos). *Emotional* is about how the purchase makes your customer feel (e.g. I feel good buying a Tesla because it's electric and I care about the environment).

Emotional and social jobs can be ripe with opportunity for businesses, because they are so often overlooked by our competitors. In their book *Jobs to Be Done*, Stephen Wunker, Jessica Wattman and David Farber observe the following:

> Emotional jobs tend to be neglected in business, especially outside the realm of consumer package goods such as food and cleaning products.... As competitors find ways to satisfy the same functional jobs at a lower price point, emotional elements can provide a vital way to differentiate your product.[10]

Do you see? Nobody buys a Rolex to tell the time. You buy a Rolex to show status (social). To show you can afford it (social). To treat yourself (emotional). To pass down an heirloom once you've popped your clogs (emotional and social). And to fit in with the rest of the Rolex-wearing crowd (social). If you just wanted to tell the time, you'd have bought a £5 watch on Amazon.

Whatever your product or your service, explore beyond the functional. Lean deep into *your* customers with JTBD in mind. You'll be onto something. I promise.

Competitors

One last thing about JTBD before we get to what questions to ask customers. Until now, you might have believed that your competitors are other businesses selling the same stuff as you. JTBD blows that theory out of the water and frames competitors as other products or services that help customers get the same job done. To revisit our watch example, a Rolex competitor could be a Louis Vuitton suitcase or a membership to an exclusive members' club in Mayfair, London – both of these fulfil some of the same social and emotional jobs our customer is after.

So what? Over to you…

1. What is your customer's real JTBD?

How to Get to Know Your Customer

2. How can you help them get it done better, quicker and easier?

Understand your customers

3. How can you reframe the way you view competitors by focusing on JTBD rather than features/pricing?

Day 5
Ask your customers

How to ask

This may seem overly simple, but 'how to ask' should be on the school curriculum. You get places when you ask, although asking is way harder for some than others. My mum taught me to ask by modelling it. Every. Damn. Day. It was excruciatingly embarrassing half the time. I had the mum who marched up to whatever authority was in question that day and requested an extension, an apology, an exception, an explanation. I hated it. Until I realized that she was right all along.

You don't need to be a full-on extrovert to ask. Asking quietly is just as effective. The most useful bit of wisdom I can impart on this matter is to ask

Ask your customers

as if your life depends on it. Thankfully, for most of us, it doesn't. But channelling that spirit can move mountains. I've done it many times. As a news reporter in crowded spaces, as a lost tourist in faraway lands and as the mother of a child who needs a pee... *now*. These days, we can ask without picking up the phone (think email, direct messages, WhatsApp, etc.). And for a lot of us, that's a good thing (phone phobia is real).

When we ask, we might get a no. We might also get a yes. Often, in fact. Most people *will* say yes if you ask for their time. Especially when you're a small business. People like small. They can relate to small (actual human beings on the other end). Once you get them talking, you'll realize that most people also like talking about themselves. And that's essentially what you want them to do. How to ask might be obvious to some. For those who can already feel the panic rising in their chest, I have a framework to calm your nerves. Follow my CAN (do) method:

- Context
    First, explain why you're asking. Educate your audience that it's good practice to ask for their input. This will set you up for future success. Tell them that you're not asking them to buy something (this is *not* a sales

call) and that you just want to understand how they go about... (insert as appropriate – e.g., doing their marketing, buying presents, relaxing, treating themselves, sorting out their finances).

- Ask
State the ask. You really care about your customers and you'd like some of their time to understand them better. Be specific with how much time you need. I'd suggest a minimum of 30 minutes and a maximum of 60 minutes (the sweet spot is probably about 45 minutes). If you plan to provide an incentive, this is the moment to tell them.

- Nitty gritty
Give as many details as you can upfront. Where do you want it to take place? Do you have a preference? Or present them with options. Being as specific as possible shows respect for the other person's time. Aim to get a yes in as few interactions as possible. 'I have availability Tuesday and Thursday between 9.30 a.m. and 12.00 p.m.' is better than a vague 'I could do anytime next week'. That

way, your customer has all the information at hand to decide quickly. You could get a date in the diary in one email exchange. Alternatively, use one of those online calendars and get people to select a date themselves.

In summary, reframe asking customers for their time as a duty of care. You're doing it so you can create stuff they'll love, find useful and want to buy. And do you know what? Almost every customer interview I've done has been enjoyable for both parties. Some have even found it cathartic (their word, not mine). As I said, people love to talk about themselves.

What to ask

Keeping JTBD in mind, let's dive into the type of questions you should ask your customers, because all the answers you need so often reside with them. Below are my golden rules for asking questions. While the goal is to use these questions (and avoid others) in customer interviews, keep them in your back pocket for when you have ad hoc encounters with your audience. In your shop, in the lift, at an event or at your local market. One good question can change everything.

How to Get to Know Your Customer

1. **Ask open-ended questions**
   Closed questions – like 'Do you enjoy outdoor swimming?' – cut conversations short and limit insights. They're great for surveys but unhelpful in real-life customer interactions. Open-ended questions – such as 'Could you tell me about the last time you went swimming outside?' – invite stories, build trust and help businesses deeply understand customer behaviours, motivations and habits.

2. **Avoid leading questions**
   Asking leading questions is easy to do, and the only way to curb this is to be aware of it and check your questions before an interview. Don't project assumptions onto your audience when asking them questions. Keep the language neutral and let customers describe their own personal experiences. You'll have more chance of getting to their truth. So, for example, instead of asking 'Is our app easy to use?' you could ask 'How would you describe using our app?'

3. **Avoid hypothetical questions**
   Asking customers if they would buy your product often produces misleading answers

Ask your customers

because the future doesn't exist yet and customers tend to tell you what you want to hear. Instead, focus on present and past behaviours: Have they bought similar products before? What did they like or dislike? This avoids the 'intention-action gap' – the discrepancy between what people say they'll do and what they actually do – and helps you gather concrete evidence to assess whether your idea meets real needs.

4. **Use the toddler technique (five whys)**
   If you've ever been in a conversation with a toddler, you'll immediately know what this means. The 'toddler technique' refers to the practice of asking 'why?' repeatedly to dig deeper into the root cause of a problem or to uncover meaningful insights. Inspired by the natural curiosity of toddlers, who often ask 'why?' in an almost endless loop, this approach challenges surface-level assumptions and encourages deeper exploration. You can get so many ideas by asking 'why?' five times. From identifying barriers to buying to generating new ideas and improvements, the toddler technique will lead you to the root cause. Always use genuine curiosity and subtle cues

to move the conversation along and dig a little deeper with each why.

5. **Measure joy and frustration**
   You can't improve what you can't measure, so we need to get better at measuring the messy stuff when we talk to customers. Asking quantifying questions helps because not all joy and not all frustration are created equal. To gauge this, focus on four areas: frustration (how painful?), time (how long and how often?), money (how much?) and success (what does good look like?). Success, like frustration, varies in significance – some achievements are expected and don't drive value, while others directly influence customer satisfaction. Always ask quantifying questions to ensure your solution targets the right problem and delivers meaningful success.

Customers go about their lives trying to get stuff done (jobs), and to do so they seek out a number of different products and services. They choose products and services not only because they fulfil a functional use (telling the time) but also because they fulfil emotional and social needs (making them look good, making them feel good). It's your job as a small business owner to ask good questions (by sticking to my golden rules) and plough all the juicy stuff you find out back into your business. Peachy. So next time you pull together a customer conversation guide, no more unplanned questions. Deal?

Getting over yourself

Despite all the tips and advice in this chapter, you might still struggle to get over the discomfort of asking. Here are a few recurring objections I come across with clients and a few ways you can overcome them. They might come in handy when your mind starts playing tricks.

- **What if I'm wrong?** What if you share your idea and nobody bites? What if you realize that you were wrong about your audience? That's learning right there. Embrace it. Better to know early and tweak accordingly than crash and burn later. Just saying.
- **What if they say no?** Will people think I'm opportunistic? Probably not. Will they think I'm trying to sell them something? Maybe (tell them you're not). Will they say no? Also maybe. Will that feel uncomfortable? Briefly.

If you're scared of a no, start with a friendly customer.

- **What if it's too late to change what I'm doing?** I get it – it's hard to turn back when you're already so far down the road. Think of this more as a detour. Remember, it's never too late to get close and personal with the people you serve.

There's no magic solution to moving through these natural feelings of discomfort. But with practice, and the tips I've given you in this chapter, you *can* get comfortable with the uncomfortable feeling of asking someone for something.

Once you have a bunch of interviews in the bag and have all your notes and transcripts, you need to make sense of it all. In research circles, we call this sense-making. It requires a bit of (colourful) kit and time, but it isn't half as painful as it sounds. Read on...

Ask your customers

✏️ So what? Over to you...

1. What's holding you back? Take six minutes to explore the reasons why you don't speak to customers. Be honest!

2. How might CAN and the five golden rules help?

Ask your customers

3. What's a great question you could ask a customer this week, and how will you do it?

Day 6
Make it make sense

Congratulations! You've done some interviews and here you are with some very valuable information on your customers – what they like, dislike and how much they are willing to pay. What now? Don't let it gather dust. This is the important bit.

Making sense of your interview insights – also called qualitative data – is part science, part art. The key is to bring just enough rigour to enable you to draw conclusions. Here, I'll share two different ways you could do it. There are other methods out there, but they all boil down to the same thing: finding repeatable ideas, patterns and trends that can help you make decisions. The method you settle on will depend on the time you have, what type of interviews you did and how your brain prefers to work. Remember: a blend of both approaches works well too.

Hypothesis tracking

Loved by start-ups for its laser-sharp properties, this will particularly suit anyone doing short, regular bursts of customer discovery. If the main purpose of your interview is to prove or disprove an assumption, this method ticks the boxes. You'll end up with something you can measure, something quantifiable (which is especially useful if you're trying to get funding or persuade other people you've found a real problem).

It's a checklist. Every time you hear your customer say something that either validates or disproves your hypothesis, you write a '1' for yes or a '0' for no. You can use this type of table as a framework to make sense of your interview notes. As you get more confident, you can do it in real time as you're speaking to customers. The spreadsheet is your friend with this method, and over time (and interviews), it will enable you to visualize your findings (tables and graphs, pivot tables if you're feeling fancy).

- **Pros:** Easy to quantify; suits shorter, targeted interviews
- **Cons:** Could miss other useful information, including context and adjacent customer challenges

Affinity mapping

This method works well after exploratory interviews. You may be fishing for new ideas, trying to understand customer behaviours and habits, or exploring challenges customers have in certain areas of their lives. With this method, you go through each interview (transcript/notes) and every time you find a noteworthy idea, you write it on a sticky note. One idea per sticky note. Write down the initials of the person you spoke to at the top of the sticky note for reference (or anonymize with Customer 1, 2, 3, etc.). At this stage, go with your gut. Don't overthink it because then you risk spiralling into endless doubt about whether the idea is interesting or not. Just write it down and stick it up on the wall (if you don't have the wall space, you can try an online tool such as Miro).

Once you've been through your interview transcripts and notes, look at all your sticky notes on the wall/floor (or leave it until your next sense-making session if you're doing it over two days). Then start grouping them by themes (themes will emerge!). At the end of the process, you'll have some clear groupings with repeatable ideas and themes. Don't forget to take a picture of all your sticky notes (just in case they fall or small hands and/or muddy paws tear them down when you're not looking).

Remember: you're not reporting to a head of insight or writing a research paper for an academic journal – you're just trying to see whether you can find any patterns in what your audience has told you.

- **Pros:** Great for visual learners; helps identify adjacent insights and opportunities
- **Cons:** Need wall space, more time-intensive

A note on outliers

When interviewing customers, you're bound to get a few curve balls. An idea or an opinion that doesn't align with what else you've been hearing. In research, we call these outliers. They tend to stick out like a sore thumb. Discard them from your sense-making unless they're about something that's interesting enough to investigate later.

Outliers are easy to spot amongst a dozen or so customer interviews, but more difficult to spot when in isolation. Remember: it's possible the feedback you receive directly from one customer could be an outlier. Always get more data before you make a decision.

Affinity mapping and hypothesis tracking are just two ways you can make sense of what customers are telling you. Next, we'll look at some other ways to gather information on customers, starting with becoming a digital spy (an ethical one, of course) from your home or office.

So what? Over to you...

1. How can you schedule time in your calendar to practise sense-making? And how can you hold yourself accountable for that?

2. Which sense-making method best suits your current goals and resources?

Make it make sense

3. Think about some recent feedback: how can you check if it's useful data or an outlier?

Day 7
Become a digital spy

If you have a bricks and mortar business, you can indulge in some real-life spying, people-watching if you like. Small businesses learn lots by observing how people browse, choose and buy in the real world. You can do this in the digital world too. But instead of watching people, you're looking at their comments, discussions, threads and conversations.

Being a digital spy

Being a digital spy is social listening (it's perfectly legal by the way). These days, people share widely (and wildly) on the internet, and we can observe. The cheapest front row seats ever. We can see what people say they want and don't want. Keep track of what they're raving about. And read the latest dirt they've dished on Trustpilot. All in their own words. With a little help from our AI friends, we can spot patterns and recurring themes that sharpen our understanding.

Where should you look?

Do an online search for 'social listening tools' and you'll be overwhelmed with results. Bigger brands use them to keep tabs on what people are saying about them, pre-empt PR disasters and get a handle on customer behaviour and sentiment. Chances are your brilliant business isn't generating the same volume of mentions online, but that doesn't mean you shouldn't listen. You want to be listening to online customer conversations and comments *within* your business area. Understanding what is delighting and pissing people off in your space.

Below are some good starting points. You'll need to set up an account to use some of these platforms, a minor inconvenience for the treasure trove of conversations you'll get in return.

- **Quora:** On this global online platform, users can ask questions and get answers on just about any topic under the sun.

- **Reddit:** This is a social news aggregation, content-rating and discussion website.
- **Amazon reviews:** For product businesses, search for similar products and check out the reviews.
- **Call-in radio shows:** This is old school and brilliant for listening to people explain their points of view in their own words.
- **Review sites:** Google reviews, Trustpilot and Yelp are a treasure trove of customer satisfaction and dissatisfaction comments.
- **Social media:** Accounts in your business area with a large following are a good place to start as they tend to get hundreds of comments.

Checking these types of platform can be quite a time-consuming process, but it's more than worth doing this on a regular basis (and not just for the memes).

Listening tools for online searches

With 8.5 billion searches typed into Google daily (that's over 90,000 every second), tapping into search engine data is another way of getting under the skin of your customers. If you knew what your customer was searching, how useful would that be? How could it help you better understand what they

Become a digital spy

need and what they're struggling with? How could it help you decide what content to create or what new offers to build?

Introducing AnswerThePublic and AlsoAsked – two useful tools that help you do just that. Powered by actual Google search data, these two platforms are a direct line into your customers' minds. Free (within reason), they do all the heavy lifting for you. You type in your relevant keywords and within seconds you're shown what people have been searching for on or around that topic. While both rely on Google, the type of data they use is different.

AnswerThePublic uses Google autocomplete data. Let's be honest, these days we rarely type in more than a couple of words in Google's search box. As soon as we start typing, Google appears to read our mind and makes a list of handy suggestions to click on instead. This list of suggestions is called autocomplete data. And it's not Google making up the suggestions. Autocomplete data stems from real (and full) searches people still make daily.

AlsoAsked aggregates data from the 'People also ask' section on the Google search results page (have a look next time you do a Google search and you'll see it as you scroll down the page). Essentially, it gives you an idea of all the other relevant and connected questions people are searching on around your selected keywords.

I suggest using AnswerThePublic in the first instance to get a broad overview of what people are searching for around your keywords. For example, if you type in business market research in AnswerThePublic, you will get results organized under headings such as Why, Can, Where, When, Will, Are, etc. Under each heading, there will be a list of questions such as: Why do businesses conduct market research? How do businesses use market research? Where to find business market research? You get the gist.

AlsoAsked is best for drilling down into a specific search query and looking at all connected questions. Results from both platforms are visual and can be downloaded in different formats. While both restrict the number of free searches, you get more than enough chances to find out something valuable.

Using AI

New tools to help businesses process and understand large customer data sets emerge all the time. The latest crop is powered by AI. ChatGPT is a prime example. This AI-powered chat bot attracted over a million users in its first five days. It's an artificial brain that speaks (think types) like a human. You can converse with it (online) and ask it questions. You can even ask it to write a blog post for your website about the benefits of buying candles (I know because I asked it to). ChatGPT has learnt everything it knows from humans and has been fed vast amounts of data written by humans.

While in desperate need of regulation (at the point of publication, this has yet to happen in the UK), AI can be a useful recourse for budget-tight and time-poor businesses. Use cases for smaller businesses are still emerging, from creating content (think the bones of your post) to processing vast amounts of qualitative data (think reviews, testimonials, interview transcripts) and derive sentiment and meaning (sense-making). One thing's for sure, these technological advances level the playing field with bigger brands, many of which have been beavering away for years developing their own AI tools.

Embrace the tools and give them a try. You've nothing to lose.

Staying on the right side of the law

Keep in mind though that just because your business is small, it's not above the law when it comes to customer data and privacy. The MRS is the industry reference when it comes to research standards, and its code of conduct governs research activities, so it's worth getting familiar with it.[11]

As we've seen, there are loads of ways to spy on customers online. Not in a creepy, unethical way, but by tapping into conversations and behaviours taking place in the digital universe. Digital spying can take many forms: reading scathing reviews from disgruntled customers, eavesdropping on chat forums or listening to people share their views on the radio. I've also shared some useful online tools to use that do the leg work for you. Now let's explore another way of understanding what your customers think: using feedback.

Become a digital spy

✏️ So what? Over to you...

1. How could you use social listening to uncover insights about your customers' needs, frustrations and desires?

2. What tool(s) might be most useful for you? Try out some of the options in this chapter.

Become a digital spy

3. How can you make this part of your regular work week?

Day 8
Stop sending shitty surveys

Businesses use surveys a lot. Too much, some might say. In this chapter, we'll look at what a survey is exactly, when to use them and how to create a really good one.

A survey is what we call a quantitative research method (as opposed to a qualitative method, such as customer interviews). You gather responses to predefined questions from a specific group of people. Responses you can quantify. Most surveys are done in person, over the phone or online. A survey feels easy – too easy. You often don't need to speak to anyone and barriers to setting one up are low, but creating a good survey is deceptively hard. Bad survey questions lead to bad data, and bad data lead to bad decisions. If you think about it, surveys by nature only give you a slice of your customer's reality, the one elicited by the predefined list of questions you ask. That said, surveys can still be a very useful tool for small businesses if you know how to create good ones.

Start with the end in mind

Whether or not you decide to use a survey will depend on *what you're trying to find out*. Don't ask anyone for anything until you know what that is. Put some thought into it or hire in some help. Otherwise, it's a waste of everyone's time. Surveys are the right method to use when you are:

- gathering demographics data to determine your audience (e.g. age, gender, nationality, residence, education, profession)
- understanding behaviours (e.g. zooming in on one or two customer behaviours and habits you want to learn more about)
- capturing in-the-moment feedback (e.g. in a shop, an airport, a restaurant, on your website)
- validating hypotheses and assumptions on a bigger scale (this can be useful after a round of customer interviews)

- evaluating customer satisfaction after a product/service has been delivered

Build surveys people fill in

Once you know what you want to find out, you need some questions. The rules are different for surveys than for customer interviews, especially when the survey is online. People are goldfishes online. If you want them to fill in your survey, you need to craft questions carefully. There's plenty written on the types of questions you can ask: the pros and cons of multiple choice, Likert scales and whatnot. Survey platforms spend a lot of time educating businesses on survey question mechanics. Super-important stuff but don't get carried away debating what type of question will elicit the best response before getting some fundamentals in place. You don't need to be like Ipsos, but you can probably improve on what you're doing now.

Ten top tips for good survey questions

1. **Be human**
   How hard can that be? From the number of robotic surveys I've seen, harder than you

think. I've seen the most humorous, warm, friendly and chatty people turn into robots the moment they write survey questions. Write as you speak.

2. **Stick (mostly) to closed questions**
   By closed questions, I mean questions that can be answered by 'yes' or 'no' or by clicking an option on a multiple-choice list. People want to get through the survey as quickly as possible. Nobody is hoping for a long survey. By all means, pepper your survey with a few open-ended questions (a question you cannot answer with a simple 'yes' or 'no') but make sure they are strategically placed.

3. **Limit the number of questions**
   The shorter the better. Seven to ten questions is the sweet spot for customer surveys (you can go shorter for pulse surveys, which will be three to four questions max on a more regular basis).

4. **Embrace smart multiple choice**
   Don't make your respondent think too much.

5. **Don't ask if you won't act**
   It's best practice in research not to ask questions if you are not going to do anything with the responses.

6. **Think beyond the survey**
   A survey is a potential recruitment tool for customer interviews. Throw in a tick box at the end with something along the lines of: 'We are always looking for customers to talk to further about our products and services. If you would like to be contacted in the future, please tick this box.' (Amend as necessary.)

7. **Incentivize**
   Everyone loves a freebie. Without breaking the bank, think about what you could do to sweeten the deal. A prize draw can work well for smaller sample sizes.

8. **Use 'other' responses**
   If you don't embrace smart multiple choice (tip 4), it's highly likely that you'll get lots of 'other' responses (because you don't know what you don't know and all that). So do everyone a favour and add a box for free text so you can learn what 'other' means.

9. **Test**
   Get your prose on point. Test for flow and typos before you press send. After a basic spell-check, rope in friends and family (the only time I'll encourage this). Ask them to fill in the survey. You'll be surprised at what a fresh pair of eyes will find.

10. **Explain and empathize**
    You're asking for people's precious time. Acknowledge and appreciate that. Tell them why you're doing a survey and what you're going to do with what you find out. You don't have to go into all the details, but offering up a little behind-the-scenes information can really help get people supporting your survey.

Work backwards

If you are struggling to word your survey questions, design consultant Erika Hall recommends working back from the type of responses that would be useful to get from your audience. Your Question Bank is another good place to start when establishing the goal of your survey. Look at the questions you've deposited. Are there any themes you can group together and ask about in a survey? One of the biggest mistakes I see with small business surveys is covering too many topics and goals in one survey. Keep your surveys tight and focused, as that increases your chances of getting results you can act on.

Now what?

You've done the survey and you have some responses. Now do something already. So many times I've filled in surveys, either in person or online, and nothing happens. Zilch. You click submit, your responses fly out into the metaverse, you never win the prize draw they lured you in with, and you never get a follow-up email to say what they did with your answers. What you do get is another 'We'd love to hear your thoughts' email six months later. We can do better than that.

This is where you take full advantage of being small. Because behind-the-scenes things will inevitably be shifting after you look at the responses. Tell people about this. 'You said, we did' messages build connections. It's powerful to show your audience that their voice counts, that they matter. If your survey is tight, with a goal and good questions, there should always be a next step.

Stop sending shitty surveys

Which platforms to use?

There are plenty of survey platforms to choose from, and seasoned surveyors will have their favourites. Here are some of the most well-known and easy-to-use platforms for small businesses. Remember: always check what data protection laws (e.g. General Data Protection Regulation, or GDPR, for the European Union) apply to your survey. Some popular platforms are:

- **Google Forms:** a free version; easy to use; unlimited surveys and responses; limited response analytics; limited design features
- **SurveyMonkey:** user-friendly for novices and pros alike; provides lots of (written) support and guidance on best practice; good response analytics; restrictions on the free version
- **Typeform:** stylish; easy to use; all about the user experience (for you and your respondents)
- **Zoho Surveys:** advanced survey analytics; offline versions; brilliant customer support; affordable; multi-language options

Please don't get blinded by design when choosing a survey platform. It's tempting to build surveys that are easy on the eye, but the most important thing will always be *why* you are doing the survey.

How to Get to Know Your Customer

When used intentionally, surveys can be a great way to understand customers, but they can also be a waste of everyone's time. Don't just send out a survey for the sake of it. Create a survey because you want to find something out and because it's the right tool for the job.

So what? Over to you…

1. How might you best use a survey in the coming weeks?

Stop sending shitty surveys

2. Try out some survey platforms. Which suits you best, and why?

3. How can you let survey respondents know what's happening as a result of their feedback?

Day 9
Test your ideas

Testing ideas doesn't have to be cumbersome. Testing doesn't have to follow a complicated process. Sometimes the doing *is* the testing, with the results helping you decide where to focus your time and when you might be onto something, or not. In this chapter, we'll explore how to test your ideas. Testing is, after all, another market research method.

Henrik Kniberg's famous 'skateboard sketch' illustrates two paths to innovation: one where the customer waits endlessly for a perfect product and another where they receive value at every step. The metaphor encourages iterative design – delivering usable, incremental products rather than holding out for perfection. Many products fail because businesses spend too long behind closed doors only to find customers have moved on.

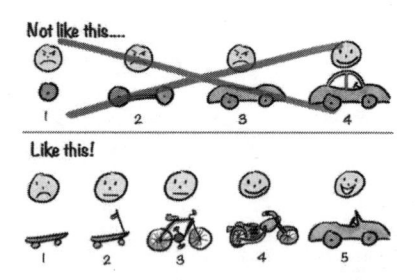

Minimum viable product by Henrik Kniberg[12]

Iterative design allows businesses to release, learn and adapt. Each version must stand alone, providing real value. Customers don't want half a car; they want one that gets them somewhere – even if not to their ultimate destination.

Testing business ideas can feel overwhelming, and small businesses should focus on quick, cost-effective methods rather than elaborate set-ups. Sometimes, just starting to test is the research itself. As innovation consultancy Strategyzer advises: 'As a rule of thumb, start cheap when uncertainty is high, and invest more as certainty grows.'[13]

Test your ideas

Practical ways to test your ideas

- **Waitlists:** Gauge demand by collecting email sign-ups for a future product. Actively promote your idea and set a target for success.
- **Ad testing:** Use Google or Facebook Ads to assess interest. Ads extend your reach but may require expert help for set-up. Positive interest can be measured through clicks or engagement.
- **Mock sales:** Test willingness to pay by creating a product page with a 'buy now' button. Notify users it's a test and offer rewards for participation. Transparency ensures trust.
- **Split testing:** Compare two variations of a web page, ad or email to see which performs better. Small sample sizes may limit clarity, so use tools and aim for adequate traffic.
- **Buy a feature:** Have customers prioritize features using a fictional budget. This highlights what they value most, whether it's for a product or service.
- **Newsletters:** Test concepts with your subscribers. They're a captive, supportive audience for feedback.

- **IRL testing:** Run small, real-world experiments, like market stalls or local workshops, to interact with your audience directly.

Always include a clear call to action that requires effort, like sign-ups or mock purchases, for stronger evidence of interest. Don't overcomplicate – start with a minimum viable product to test your idea quickly and effectively (think skateboard...).

Testing price

Pricing can be tricky, even for large businesses. Don't simply ask customers: 'How much would you pay?' This often leads to low-ball responses. Instead, test willingness to pay with a pricing range customers can react to.

Start by combining internal insights (costs and margins) with external market research. Compare your pricing against that of two or three competitors, then decide if you'll position yourself as budget, mid-market or premium.

For deeper insights, explore pricing survey methods like the Gabor-Granger method (step-by-step price testing) or Van Westendorp's price sensitivity analysis. Both can help determine optimal pricing; both are much less complicated than they

Test your ideas

sound. They help businesses test willingness to pay and assess the optimum value (and price) customers place on a product or service. Both consist of asking respondents a series of simple questions.

The Gabor-Granger survey asks respondents to say whether they'd pay for your offer at a set price. For example: Would you pay £50 for this? Yes/no. If the respondent says yes, then you move up a price level: Would you pay £60 for this? Yes/no. And so on. At scale, and with the relevant audience, you get to the optimum price. You can use the Gabor-Granger method for testing price increases on existing products, new pricing for an improved product or testing price for offers under £25.

The Van Westendorp method, on the other hand, extracts price sensitivity and the relationship between customer perception of quality and price. It's best used for higher-value items or brand-new products and services. It uses four questions to determine the optimum price:

1. At what price would this product be so expensive you wouldn't consider it?
2. At what price would this product be so cheap you'd feel the quality is poor?
3. At what price would this product start to get expensive enough that you'd still consider

buying it but you'd have to give it some thought?
4. At what price would you feel this product is a bargain and great value for money?

You can find both methodologies online and set up your own survey, but if you are going to do it alone, here are a few things to watch out for:

- **Sample size:** For this to be effective, you need to have a decent online sample (100+ people). If you don't have that kind of audience, consider using a third party who can set the survey up for you and access a wider, targeted audience to ensure statistical relevance.
- **Offer:** For both methods, you need to accurately describe and position the offer you are testing.
- **Price points:** You need to have a price range in mind before you set up your survey.

Testing early and often reduces risks and builds confidence step by step, iteration by iteration. Like a diligent dung beetle, meticulously rolling its pungent prize down a hill. Testing can be lightweight, and remember that sometimes the *doing* is the testing. Hopefully, this chapter has boosted your pricing confidence. Businesses need good pricing, and good

Test your ideas

pricing comes from being more intentional and taking full advantage of the tools at our disposal.

> ### ✏️ So what? Over to you...
>
> 1. How might small, usable versions of your intended product or service provide immediate benefits to customers?

2. Which of the testing methods could you use to future-proof your business ideas?

Test your ideas

3. How might you go about testing your pricing over the coming days/weeks?

Day 10
Turn insights into action

So, how do you go from reading this book to making market research happen in your business? It needs to be pragmatic and doable. Otherwise, it won't happen. (I know because I'm a small business too!) In this last step, I provide just one approach for how to do just that: start small and solid (there are more in my book, *Do Penguins Eat Peaches?*, or online at: www.productjungle.co.uk/resources). This is not prescriptive, and you don't need to follow it by the letter. Pick 'n' mix and amend and tweak as you see fit. But it's always better to start with something. It's how change (however small) happens.

Turn insights into action

Start small and solid

- Commit to sending at least one survey a year. It could be to a subset of your community.
- Schedule two desk research sessions in your calendar. Carve out the time in advance (that means it's more likely to happen!). Sessions can be between 30 and 60 minutes. Save relevant reports and insights in your Market Research folder (go create one already!).
- Once every three months, fire up some of the tools and sites I recommend and get customer eavesdropping.
- Commit to conducting at least one annual exploratory customer interview sprint.[14] Open your diary and schedule it three to six months in advance. Think about it as separate blocks of time: time to decide on a high-level goal; time to craft questions; time to find folks to speak to; time to conduct the interviews; and time to make sense of it all.
- Check out the different tests you could run (see Day 9).
- Create an online or offline folder or document called Question Bank. Every time you start wondering something about your audience,

bank the question. Your deposits can fuel your surveys and interviews.

When to hire the pros

We've focused here on what you can do yourself. But there will be situations when calling in expertise is the right thing to do. Investing in professional market research support can accelerate discovery and get you reliable answers faster. It can help navigate hard-to-reach audiences, negotiate different cultures and markets, and increase your chances of survey success with skilfully crafted questions.

Here are a few situations where you might consider calling in some pro help:

- **Investment:** If you are looking to raise *serious* money from investors (or the bank), you'll need to show you've done some homework on customers. Having support from a research professional ensures you get the right insights, in the right format, to reassure investors you *know* what makes your customers tick.
- **Marketing and branding:** Copywriting for your website, ads or offers is difficult to get right alone. If your copy isn't generating the results you expected, it might be time to seek

professional help. Good copywriters will always start with your customer.
- **New launch:** The more money you plan to invest in launching something, the greater the risk of losing it if you get things wrong. Do yourself a favour and get the help you need if you are thinking *big* big.
- **New market:** Imagine you want to enter the Chinese market. Unless you're a Chinese market expert, you'll need some help. Same for any other new market you wish to enter. It will avoid costly mistakes down the line.
- **Large surveys:** If you need a large sample size, survey specialists can help get your questions in front of the right audience. They can also make sure you get the most out of your questions.
- **Discussion guide:** Sometimes we just need a little support crafting quality questions. Some independent market research specialists can support with making sure you get the most out of your customer interviews (brilliant questions = better insights).

Investing in professional help doesn't mean washing your hands of the whole process. Stay as close as you can and listen in to conversations where possible, even if someone else is interviewing. Keep tabs on data coming in. Remember that customer insights are always more powerful when they are first-hand. Finally, choosing the right partner needn't be daunting. After reading this book, you have a solid enough idea of what good research looks like.

Here are a few questions I recommend you ask if, and when, you select a market research partner for your business:

- Have you worked with small businesses in the past?
- What experience do you have working with my type of target customer/industry?
- What types of insights did you deliver and in what format?
- How do you go about recruiting participants/accessing audiences?
- How will I know that you are targeting the right people?
- What will the project deliverables look like?
- What feedback do you give on my research goal?

To sum up

You now have everything you need to start getting to know your customer better, and that has the potential to transform your business. Start listening, and take action!

> ### ✏️ So what? Over to you...
>
> 1. Pick one of those action points and get started!

Conclusion

In business, as in life, there are no guarantees. Everything is always shifting. People. Culture. The economy. Ourselves. It's called impermanence. Market research as a practice can be an anchor to tether you back to a repeatable practice. A practice that gets you one step closer to your customers, to the people you serve. Because without them, there is no business. If you're not probing, poking, asking and checking (more of the time), you're guessing.

Market research doesn't have to be perfect. Understanding customers never is. Customers are humans. They are messy, flawed, unpredictable and irrational. But with the right mindset, intention, tools and skills, you *can* make sense of them. Enough sense to make better decisions. To move forward with more clarity. To fail faster and create stuff that people want and buy. You won't ever have all the answers, but each time you lean in, you'll *get* a few more. Tori Rosevink, Chief Insight Officer at Categoracle, summed it up perfectly: 'There's not one *right* way to

Conclusion

do market research. The only wrong way is not to do it at all.'

Running a small business, being your own boss, freelancing and making a living from it is hard work. Far from being another item on the never-ending to-do list, let market research relieve some of the burden. Think of the ten steps in this book as your map in the maze. Even with the map in your hand, you're still bound to take a few wrong turns, but you'll make it out faster than if you were without it.

So, stay curious. Bank those questions. Be brave. Keep leaning in to your customers. In these turbulent times, the answers so often lie with them. But we need to ask.

I hope these steps help you feel a little wiser, a little braver and a little more curious. Do tell me how you get on.

Endnotes

[1] C. Doyle, 'Spread the word' in *Impact*, 38, p. 3 (July 2022).

[2] L. Burnam, *32 user experience research statistics to win over stakeholders*, User Interviews (February 2023). Available from: www.userinterviews.com/blog/15-user-experience-research-statistics-to-win-over-stakeholders-in-2020.

[3] S. Blank and B. Dorf, *The Startup Owner's Manual* (2020).

[4] Blank and Dorf, *The Startup Owner's Manual*, p. 56.

[5] Oxford Learners Dictionaries, *Assumption*. Available from: www.oxfordlearnersdictionaries.com/definition/english/assumption?q=assumption.

[6] W. Berliner, '"Schools are killing curiosity": why we need to stop telling children to shut up and learn', *The Guardian* (28 January 2020). Available from: www.theguardian.com/education/2020/jan/28/schools-killing-curiosity-learn.

[7] Z. Neale Hurston, *Dust Tracks on a Road* (1996), p. 143.

[8] Blank and Dorf, *The Startup Owner's Manual*.

[9] D. Smith, 'Proof! Just six degrees of separation between us' in *The Guardian* (3 August 2008). Available from: www.theguardian.com/technology/2008/aug/03/internet.email.

Endnotes

[10] S. Wunker, J. Wattman and D. Farber, *Jobs to Be Done: A roadmap for customer-centered innovation* (2017), pp. 31–32.

[11] MRS, *Code of Conduct* (May 2023). Available from: www.mrs.org.uk/standards/code-of-conduct.

[12] H. Kniberg, *Making sense of MVP (minimum viable product) – and why I prefer earliest testable/usable/lovable*, blog.crisp.se (25 January 2016). Available from: https://blog.crisp.se/2016/01/25/henrikkniberg/making-sense-of-mvp, reproduced here under Creative Commons. https://www.crisp.se/konsulter/henrik-kniberg/faq.

[13] A. Osterwalder, Y. Pigneur, G. Bernarda and A. Smith, *Value Proposition Design* (2014), p. 216.

[14] A sprint is a predefined length of time when you commit to getting something done (taken from agile software methodology).

Enjoyed this?
Then you'll love…

Do Penguins Eat Peaches? And other unexpected ways to discover what your customers want

Business Book Awards 2024: Highly Commended

Why are customers so damn fickle? They say one thing, do the other. They change their minds. Give you false hopes. Keep you guessing. But without them, there is no business.

Finding out what your customers want needn't be potluck. *Do Penguins Eat Peaches?* demystifies big-business market research tools, tips and tricks for you, the smaller business. With smaller budgets. Smaller teams. Those of you who want to do right by your customers but need a little help with the how.

From sending smart surveys and asking quality questions to desk research and the rise of social

Enjoyed this? Then you'll love...

listening, this book teaches you how to discover what your customers want.

Katie Tucker is an inspirational product leader with over 12 years' experience leading teams and delivering stand-out products and services. In 2020 she founded Product Jungle, helping hundreds of businesses understand customers better. She is also a mentor, speaker and the pen behind the popular newsletter *Jungle Juice*.

Other 6-Minute Smarts titles

Building Great Teams (based on *Workshop Culture* by Alison Coward)

Do Change Better (based on *How to be a Change Superhero* by Lucinda Carney)

How to be Happy at Work (based on *My Job Isn't Working!* by Michael Brown)

Mastering People Management (based on *Mission: To Manage* by Marianne Page)

No-Nonsense PR (based on *Hype Yourself* by Lucy Werner)

Present Like a Pro (based on *Executive Presentations* by Jacqui Harper)

Reimagine Your Career (based on *Work/Life Flywheel* by Ollie Henderson)

Sales Made Simple (based on *More Sales Please* by Sara Nasser Dalrymple)

The Listening Leader (based on *The Listening Shift* by Janie van Hool)

The Speed Storytelling Toolkit (based on *Exposure* by Felicity Cowie)

Write to Think (based on *Exploratory Writing* by Alison Jones)

Look out for more titles coming soon! Visit www.practicalinspiration.com for all our latest titles.